MARIAM SHIT

BECAUSE OF YOU

A **POETRY** COLLECTION

BECAUSE OF YOU

Designed & Published in Nigeria by
TEBEBA Global Publishing Ltd.

PUBLISHER'S CONTACT:
www.tebeba.com
Info@tebeba.com

Dedication

For my late Mother,

Wuraola Fehintola Shittu,

who showed me what love is and isn't.

I miss you, Mama.

Acknowledgements

Many thanks to my family and friends for their endless support and encouragement through this journey. Writing is a skill I stumbled upon, and if I didn't have you guys always rooting for me, I wonder if I'll be here today. I've come to appreciate poetry in all its versions and greatness. I'm genuinely grateful to you all for indulging and engaging in my self-discovery.

To my social media community, WordPress family and everyone else that may have supported my writing in one way or another, from the beginning or recently, thank you.

This is for us.

Love

Send love.
Show love.
Share love.
Give love.
Be love.

Contents

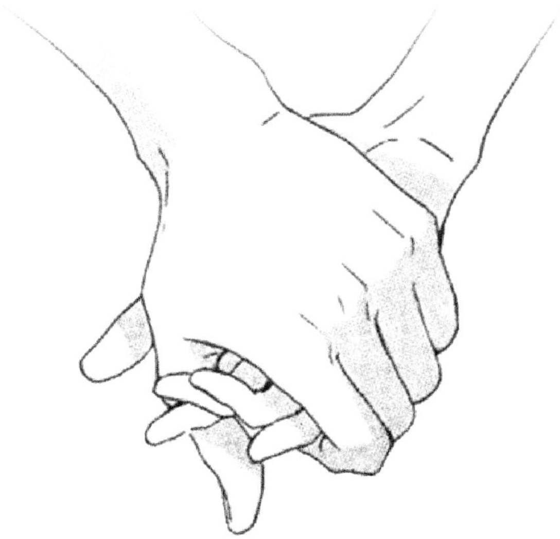

This Kind of Love

I want a love
that lights up my life

That asks questions
and believes the answers
That listens to understand
and remembers when necessary

That makes love
and not war
That cherishes what we have
and knows every day will not be rosy

That forgives
and will never give up on us
That doesn't shove the word love
but shows it instead

That doesn't control
but advises and supports
That understands the value of growth
and takes gradual steps to achieve it

That brings endless joy
and makes me feel safe
That will always be there
and grow old with me

I want a love
that is this kind of love

My Desire

My desire
is to
meet you
love you
choose you
and be with you
at 11:59pm every new year's eve

All I Saw Was You

The dancefloor wasn't empty
but all I saw was you
as our hearts glided
to the rhythm of love
and our bodies swayed
to the rhythm of the night

Crazy With You

I don't care if this is new
I don't care if this is fast
I don't care if this is crazy
I want to be crazy with you

I'll Be Waiting

When day turns to night
And the stars light up the sky
I'll be waiting for you to come by
Behind the yellow light

Promise Me

Promise me
that your love is true
that you know what you want
that I will always be enough
that you have unquestionable faith in us
and I will never have a reason to look back

Promise me
that you mean everything you say
that I'll never cry myself to sleep because of you
that when love fails us, we'll still be kind to each other
that we'll weather our storms together
and be together forever

Promise me

If This Is Love

I see you
Walking towards me
I'm grinning
Checking you out

Butterflies in my belly
While you're with me
We kiss
And you take my breath away

If this is love
I don't want it to end...

I'm here alone
But you're in my thoughts
I yearn for my medicine
That is what you are

We talk
And I forget all my worries
Your voice
Is music to my soul

If this is love
I'm glad I found it...

I feel safe
Knowing I have you by me
When I'm with you
I can see us together grey and old

I'm content
Knowing I have the best
When I'm not with you
I can't stop thinking about you

I hope this is love
I want it forever

New Love

I love new love
Nothing else matters
temporarily

Choose Me

Choose me
teach me
guide me
believe in me

Call me
comfort me
protect me
show me love

Fight me
encourage me
understand me
correct my wrong

Commend me
take me higher
be patient with me
make me stronger

And help me be the best person I can be

A Thousands Times

A thousand times,
I wondered about this day.

A thousand times,
I prayed for this moment.

A thousand times,
I rehearsed what I was going to say.

A thousand times,
I imagined how things will turn out.

but meeting you exceeded my expectations,
a thousand times.

I'll Let You In

I'll show you
how to love me
so you will know
how to please me
and never fail me

I'll let you
see the real me
flaws and all me

I'll let you
see me
in a way
no one else has
I'll let you in

Your Heart Chose Me

Darling,
I'm happy
your heart
chose me

We Were Meant To Be

Before I met you
I had seen you in my dreams
creepy or not
I know we were meant to be

I Believe In Love Again

You've made me believe
that love exists again
and if that's the only thing
I get out of this
I won't mind
because it's enough

You & I

Let's
act like no one's watching
love like nothing else matters
dance like we've got the best moves
live like we have all the time in the world

Love Is You

I don't need to
listen to another love song
to tell me what love is
because
you have shown me that
love is you

In You

In You
I found purpose
You made me dream again

In You
I found hope
You made me believe again

In You
I found comfort
You made me feel safe again

In You
I found beauty
You made me see again

In You
I found joy
You made me want to live again

In You
I found love
You made me give my all again

In You
I found happiness
You made me laugh again

In You
I found peace
You made me whole again

So don't go breaking my heart

Love Is Always There

When you breathe
When you smile
When you laugh
When you cry

Love is always there, even if you don't feel it.

Love Found Me

I wasn't trying to be seen
but you still came my way

I wasn't looking for this
but now I think of us

I wasn't searching for love
but somehow it found me

We All Need Love

Just as a plant
needs water
to survive
and a business
needs money
to thrive

We all need
support
encouragement
appreciation
and love
to shine

I Don't Care

I don't care
if it's too early
I know how I feel
I love you
and it's okay
if you don't feel
the same way too

Please Be Mine

I'm writing this
to let you know
that no day passes by
without you on my mind
So I'll be thinking of you
this valentine's day
like I do every day
Please, be mine.

How I Know You Know Love

I see it
in the way you
look at me
talk to me
care for me
and push me

I feel it
in the way you
listen to me
give to me
choose me
and want more for me

I see it
in the way you
show me
I come first
and that's how
I know you love me

I Love How You Love Me

I love
how you make me see
sides of me
I didn't know existed

I love
how you open my eyes
to a world
of possibilities

I love
how you love me

Like A Baby

I sleep like a baby at night
knowing I have you
to conquer all my excuses, pain and storms with

When It Comes To Love

When it comes to love
I give it all my heart
and everything I've got
because when it comes to love
it comes to you first
and every other thing is next

True Love

It isn't crushing
It isn't confusing
It isn't assuming
It isn't misleading

It never dies
It never withers
It never abuses
It never changes

It is kind
It is gentle
It is honest
It is forgiving

It is unshakable
It is unbreakable
It is irreplaceable
It is unforgettable

It is true love

Maybe, Just Maybe

Maybe
just maybe
this time will be different

Maybe
just maybe
you will be my end and my beginning

Maybe
just maybe
I will conquer the world with you by my side

Perfect

I thought it was impossible to have perfect days
but my days have been perfect, since you came along.

She's Sure

She's sure
She's happy
She's in love

In Love

I've never seen a sky this blue
or a heart this true
I've never been in love this soon
and I adore its tune

My Actions

My words will never be enough
to express my love for you
So I will focus on my actions
To show you I'll always be there for you

I Love You More Than You Know

I love you
more than
my words can say
and actions can show

I love you
more than
everything I own
and every person I know

I love you
more than
you will ever know

My Favourite

You're my favourite
Favourite song
Favourite thing
Favourite story
Favourite place
Favourite taste
Favourite person

My Favourite Place

My favourite place in the world
is wherever you are

My Eternal Love

Someone once told me
to always say how I feel
because waiting never helps
So here goes:
I want you today,
tomorrow
now,
and always

Hot & Cold

You keep me cool but you also set my heart on fire

The Interpreter

I love that I'm the only one
that understands what you say
when you talk with your eyes

Even When You're Mad

Hug me
Hold me
Kiss me
Love me
Care for me
even when you're mad

What It Means To Love

I heard every relationship has secrets,
but ours will be nothing like that.
We'll show the world,
what it means to love.

For You

I hate football
but I'd watch a game or two
just to be with you

I hate reading
but I'd read a book you like
to review it with you

I hate driving
but I'd take the wheel
for you

For You #2

I'll travel the world
swim in the deepest oceans
climb the highest mountains
and keep my fears at bay
just to be with you

When It Comes To You

I know emotions cloud logic
but when it comes to you
I don't mind being stupid
stupidly in love

Every Moment With You

Every moment with you
feels like freshly laid sheets,
strawberries dipped in chocolate,
my birthday, and multiple hugs

When I'm With You

I've never felt
more alive
than I do
when I'm with you

I've never felt
more like myself
than I have
when I'm with you

I've never felt
more at peace
like I feel
when I'm with you

Nothing On You

butterflies and flowers
champagne and dessert
my first and my ex
got nothing on you

The Little Things You Do

foot rubs
bear hugs
date nights
forehead kisses
belly runs
free lunches
weekend massages
late night phone calls

The little things are not little, when they're done by you

I've Always Needed You

I thought I had no needs
but since you came my way
I've been a bundle of needs
And the closer I get to you
I realize I've always needed you

I Have You

Everything I want
won't belong to me
and that's okay
because I already have you

I Choose You

In a world full of darkness,
I found light in you.

In a world full of pain,
I found joy in you.

In a world full of hate,
I chose to love you.

When It's You

I hate it when people call me sweetheart,
but I don't mind when it's you calling.

I hate it when people keep me waiting,
but I don't mind when it's you I'm waiting on.

I hate it when I'm on the phone for hours,
but I don't mind when it's you.

My Love For You

My love for you is strong
It will never fade, no matter how long
My love for you will never end
It will stay strong and never bend

Like A Baby

I sleep like a baby at night
knowing I have you
to conquer all my excuses, pain and storms with

My Many Names

Sweetheart.
Sunshine.
Darling.
Beautiful.
Babe.
All the names I answer when it's you calling.

We Go Together

We go together
like gin and tonic
cheese and crackers
movies and popcorn
Sundays and brunch
And a jacket on a cold night

My Snacks

I like my snacks
a little bit sweet
a little bit savory
crispy and moist
just like you

Picture Perfect

If I could paint a picture of the life I want,
I'll choose lots of sunshine
rainbows and butterflies.

I'll choose lots of laughter
peace and joy.

I'll choose lots of love
meaningful friendships and relationships
not forgetting Prince Charming and happily ever after.

If I could paint a picture
of the life I want,
I'll choose you.

Consume Me

I want to drown in your existence
feel your every being
breathe the air you breathe
feel every inch of your body
let your wholeness consume me

Tell Me

It's never too late
to say how you feel
It's never too early
to show me you care
any time of the day is okay
to tell me you need me

Love Me

find me
save me
heal me
love me

Love Me Naked

love me right
love me tender
love me hard
love me now
love me naked

I Promise

I’ve said the words
“I promise”
often
and I may have
broken some promises
along the line
but I’m certain
a lifetime with you
is a promise
I will never break

I love love

I love loving you
I love thinking about you
I love feeling loved by you
I love being in love with you
I love love

I Love Him

I don't have to say too much
it always shows

I don't have to do too much
he always knows

I still want to though
because I love him so

You

You are the magic
I never knew
I wanted
but always needed

You are the star
that shines
brightest
in the dark

You are the happiness
I've grown to
treasure more
every single day

You are my today, tomorrow and forever.

You #2

Entirely,
Assertedly,
Undisputedly,
You.

You Know Me

You always find
a solution
to every problem.

You always know
what to say
to make it all okay.

You always show up
no matter
the time or place.

You always get me,
even when
I don't get myself.

You always know,
because
you know me.

You Are Always On My Mind

When the sun comes up
and its light is in my path

When I hear a song I love
and its sweet melody fills my ears

When I'm on a winning streak
and my heart is leaping with joy

When the day's work is over
and I begin my journey home

When darkness replaces light
and the stars sparkle bright

When life tests me
and it seems impossible to go on

When the scars fade
and I'm no longer afraid

You're always on mind and always there.

You Are Peace

When I look into your eyes, I see peace.

Safe

There were no stars in the sky
There was darkness all around me
There was no one here but you
And somehow
I knew you were enough
I knew I was safe with you

Safe With You

I've never
felt the need
to pretend to you
because I know
all my sides
are safe with you

I've never
felt the need
to hide from you
because I know
all my secrets
are safe with you

I've never
felt the need
to look elsewhere
because I know
I'm safe with you

You Are Home

You're my truth
You're my strength
You're my escape
You're my peace
You are home

You Are My Light

You make me look for the rainbow in a thunderstorm
You make me look for stars in the sky on a sunny day
You make me find light in the dark
You make me find peace in chaos
You make me see possible where it seems impossible
You make me see greatness
You make me unstoppable

Everything Is You

I see you in everything.
Everything is you.

I see you in everything,

In the blouse I choose to wear to work
and the food I eat during the day

In the music I listen to on my way home
and the scent that greets me when I open the door

In the stranger's face I pass by on my evening walk
and the darkness when I turn off the lights to sleep.

Everything is you.

The Way That I Love You

All my life
I thought I knew
what love was
but then I met you
and realized
I have never
truly loved anyone
the way that I love you

My Love For You #2

As certain as you are
that the birds will chirp
every morning

So am I certain that
my love for you will renew
every morning

As certain as you are
that you grow older
every second

So am I certain that
my love for you
will never stunt

As certain as you are
that light will break
every morning

So am I certain that
my love for you
will never die

My Wish

If I met a genie today
and he granted me three wishes
I'll wish to spend eternity with you three times.

Because You Love Me

Wake me up with breakfast in bed
because you want to feed me

send me roses at work
because you know I love them

Buy me a dress
because you think it'll fit perfectly

Book me a spa day
because you think I need it

Buy us front row tickets to a concert
because you know the artiste is my favorite

Call me during the day
because you want to hear my voice

give me a foot rub
because I had a long day

Pick up the groceries
because you want to take the burden off me

Do all of this and more
because you love me

We Are One

Everything that
belongs to me
belongs to you
I live for you
I breathe you
We are one

Our Love

Our love is like the sun
It soothes and it burns
It's always there
and it has no competition in the galaxy

Our love is like fire
It's hot and fierce
It's always lit
and it purifies everything it touches

Our love is like music
It pleases and it heals
It's always alive
and it transforms the universe

Our love is like friendship
It isn't perfect
but it's always safe
and it's all I'll ever need

Only You

Its been you
Only you

When I wake up in the morning
and I see the light
When I go to bed at night
and darkness surrounds me

I think of you
Only you

When the stars are missing
and the sky is at its darkest
When the rain is pouring
and its sound is deafening

I long for you
Only you

When I hear good news
and I'm leaping with joy
When things aren't going well
and I'm crushing inside

I look for you
Only you

When my mind wanders
and I can't tame my heavy heart
When the world feels small
and I wonder if I belong here

I remember you
Only you

It has always been you
It will always be you
Only you

All That You Are, My Love

You're the air in my lungs
You're my rain in drought
You're my water in the desert
You're the stillness in my heart

You're my coffee in the morning
You're the rainbow in my sky
You're my jacket on a cold evening
You're the cure to my pain

You're my best friend
You're my cheerleader
You're my happiness
You're my home

Where I Belong

Wherever you are in the world is where I belong

When I Fall

When I fall
into a million pieces
I'm glad I have you
to make me whole again

I'm Yours

Just in case
you didn't already know
I'm yours today, tomorrow and forevermore

Together

I hope we'll
learn together
give together
play together
try together
cry together
laugh together
worry together
plan together
travel together
make life changing decisions together
suffer consequences together
teach together
create together
share together
pray together
change together
grow together
and live together, forever

Forever Mine

As gold never turns to rust
Our love will never become lust

As long as I have air in my lungs
I won't give you up like my pie crust

Forever And Always

In the rain or the sun
In the dark or the light

In trouble or in peace
In despair or in joy

I want you with me.

Always

We may be miles apart,
but you are always in my heart.

It's Always You

In the light
In the dark

In the bloom
In the gloom

In quiet
In chaos

It's always you on my mind

I Always Think Of You

On my loud days
and quiet days

On my happy days
and sad days

On my basic days
and remarkable days

I always think of you

My Muse

You will always be
the ink in my pen
the voice in my head
the words on my notepad
and the beat of my heart

A Letter To You

I love the way
I smile at the mirror
when I'm thinking of you

I love the way
my eyes light up
when I see a call from you

I love the way
everything feels right
when I hear your voice

I love the way
I'm at peace
when I'm with you

I love the way
I still want you
even when things get tough

I love the way
I'm certain
about doing forever with you

Thank You

Thank you for loving me
Thank you for guiding me
Thank you for teaching me
Thank you for correcting me
Thank you for forgiving me
Thank you for defending me
Thank you for protecting me
Thank you for encouraging me
Thank you for accommodating me
Thank you for entertaining me
Thank you for spoiling me
Thank you for choosing me

Let's Set A Date

Let's set a date
It's time, no need to wait
to change my name
and accept my fate
You're mine and I'm yours
for hundred years times eight

It's My Day

It's been a long time coming
The day is finally here
My day
A day I'm not sharing

Everyone is here for me
Well, for us
My day
A day I feel special

My name is on everyone's lips
Well, our names
My day
A day I will always remember

I am dancing away my sorrows
Happy to start my forever
My day
A day I bear a new name

I am crying tears of joy
Looking around in awe
My day
A day I feel happiest

All my friends are here
To stare and wish me well
My day
A day I look the prettiest

I'm happy I found you
I can't stop smiling
My day
A day I have no worries

Two have become one
I'm glad I chose you
Our day
A day we get our happily ever after

Because of You

It may seem like
I always have the words
for every mood
every feeling
every action
and every situation

It may seem like
I always know
what to say
and what not to say
to make it all okay

But
it's because of you
that my words
have found meaning
so thank you
for believing in me

Author's Note

Every poem in this book is a reflection of my thoughts, feelings and wishes.
I hope my words bring you joy, comfort and healing.
I hope my words bring you peace.
I hope my words bring you love.
I hope you find your YOU.

ABOUT THE AUTHOR

Born and raised in Lagos, Nigeria, Mariam Shittu is a writer, content creator and Human Resource Professional. She holds a B.Sc. degree in Industrial Relations and Personnel Management from University of Lagos and a Professional Diploma in Human Resource Management. Her deepest yearning for arts led her into the world of creativity in 2017, when she started sharing her writings with the world through her blog. Visit her at www.mariamshittu.com. Because of You is her first book.